MY FAVORITE DRAWING PAD FOR KIDS

MY DRAWING SKETCHBOOK

This Drawing Pad Belongs to:

_____

Sketch - Draw - Doodle

I FEEL HAPPY TODAY!

Sketch – Draw – Doodle

I FEEL PLAYFUL TODAY!

Sketch – Draw – Doodle

I FEEL AWESOME TODAY!

Sketch – Draw – Doodle

I FEEL GREAT TODAY!

Sketch - Draw - Doodle

I FEEL CREATIVE TODAY!

Sketch - Draw - Doodle

I FEEL INSPIRED TODAY!

Sketch – Draw – Doodle

I FEEL COOL TODAY!

Sketch – Draw – Doodle

I FEEL STRONG TODAY!

Sketch – Draw – Doodle

I FEEL GRATEFUL TODAY!

Sketch - Draw - Doodle

I FEEL SMART TODAY!

Sketch – Draw – Doodle

I FEEL AWESOME TODAY

Sketch – Draw – Doodle

I FEEL CREATIVE TODAY!

Sketch – Draw – Doodle

I FEEL HAPPY TODAY!

Sketch - Draw - Doodle

I FEEL BLESSED TODAY!

Sketch - Draw - Doodle

I FEEL COOL TODAY!

Sketch – Draw – Doodle

I FEEL SMART TODAY!

Sketch – Draw – Doodle

I FEEL PLAYFUL TODAY!

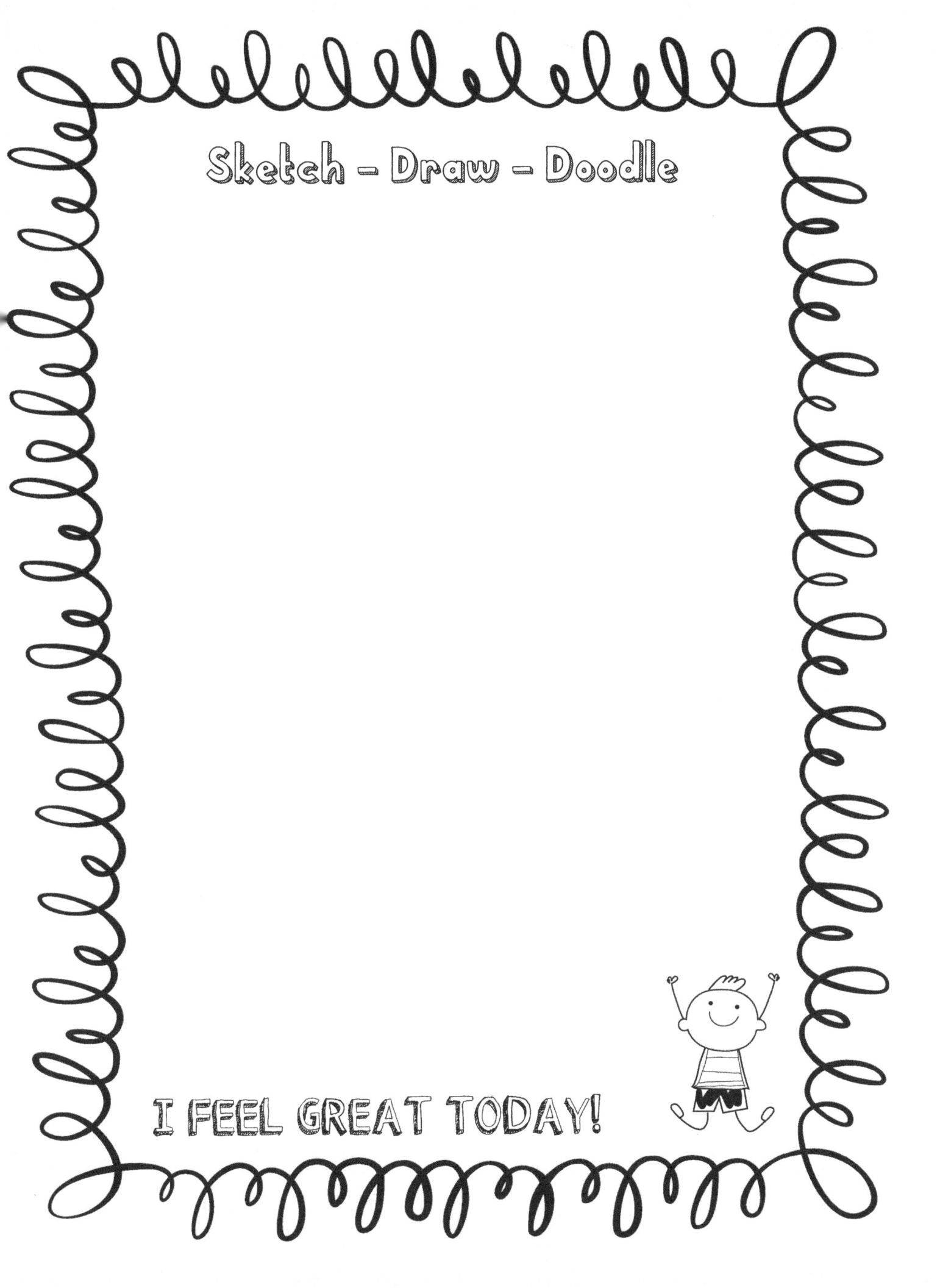

Sketch – Draw – Doodle

I FEEL GREAT TODAY!

Sketch – Draw – Doodle

I FEEL HAPPY TODAY!

Sketch - Draw - Doodle

I FEEL COOL TODAY!

Sketch - Draw - Doodle

I FEEL CREATIVE TODAY!

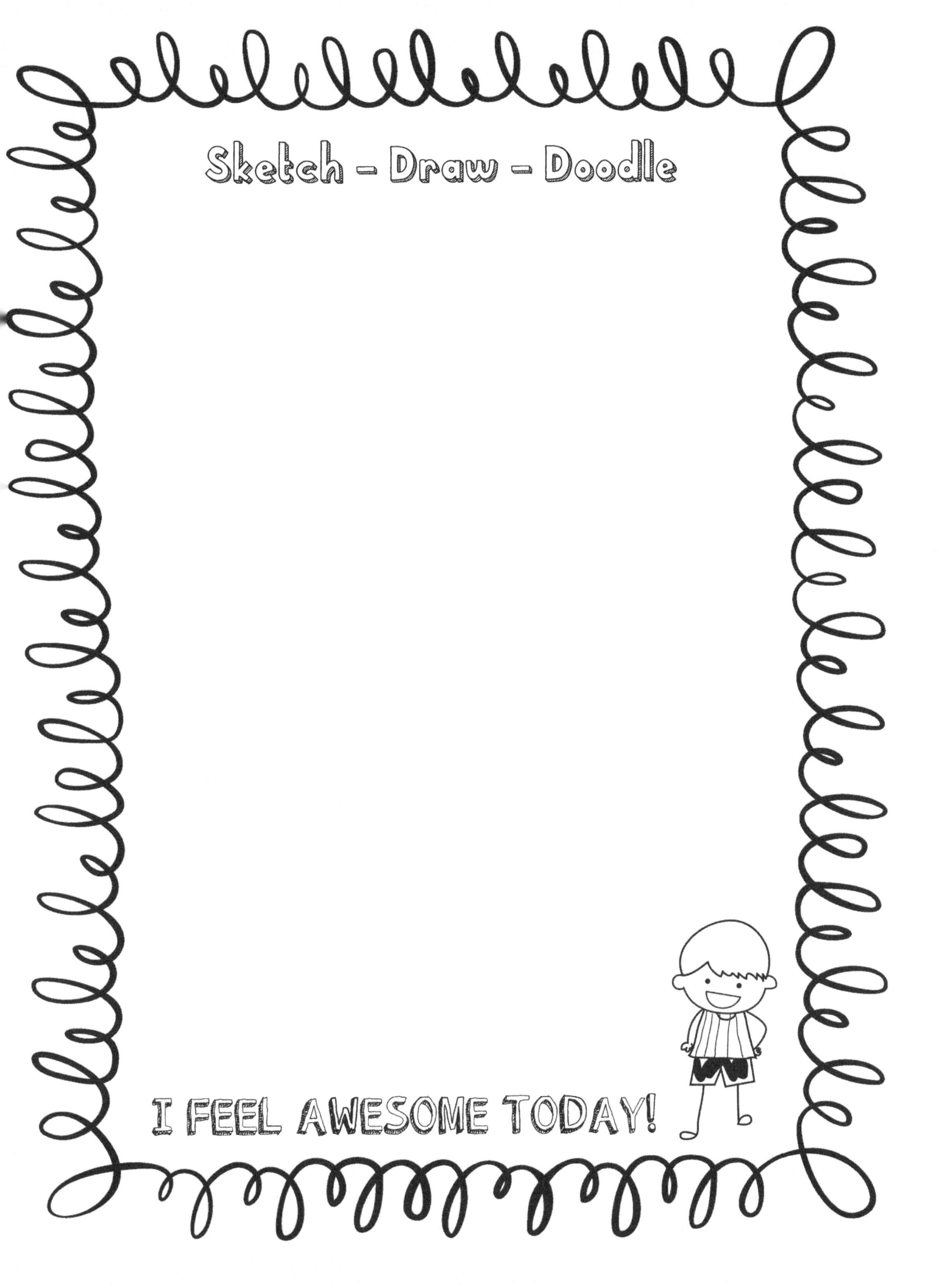

Sketch - Draw - Doodle

I FEEL AWESOME TODAY!

Sketch – Draw – Doodle

I FEEL THANKFUL TODAY!

Sketch - Draw - Doodle

I FEEL COOL TODAY!

Sketch - Draw - Doodle

I FEEL STRONG TODAY!

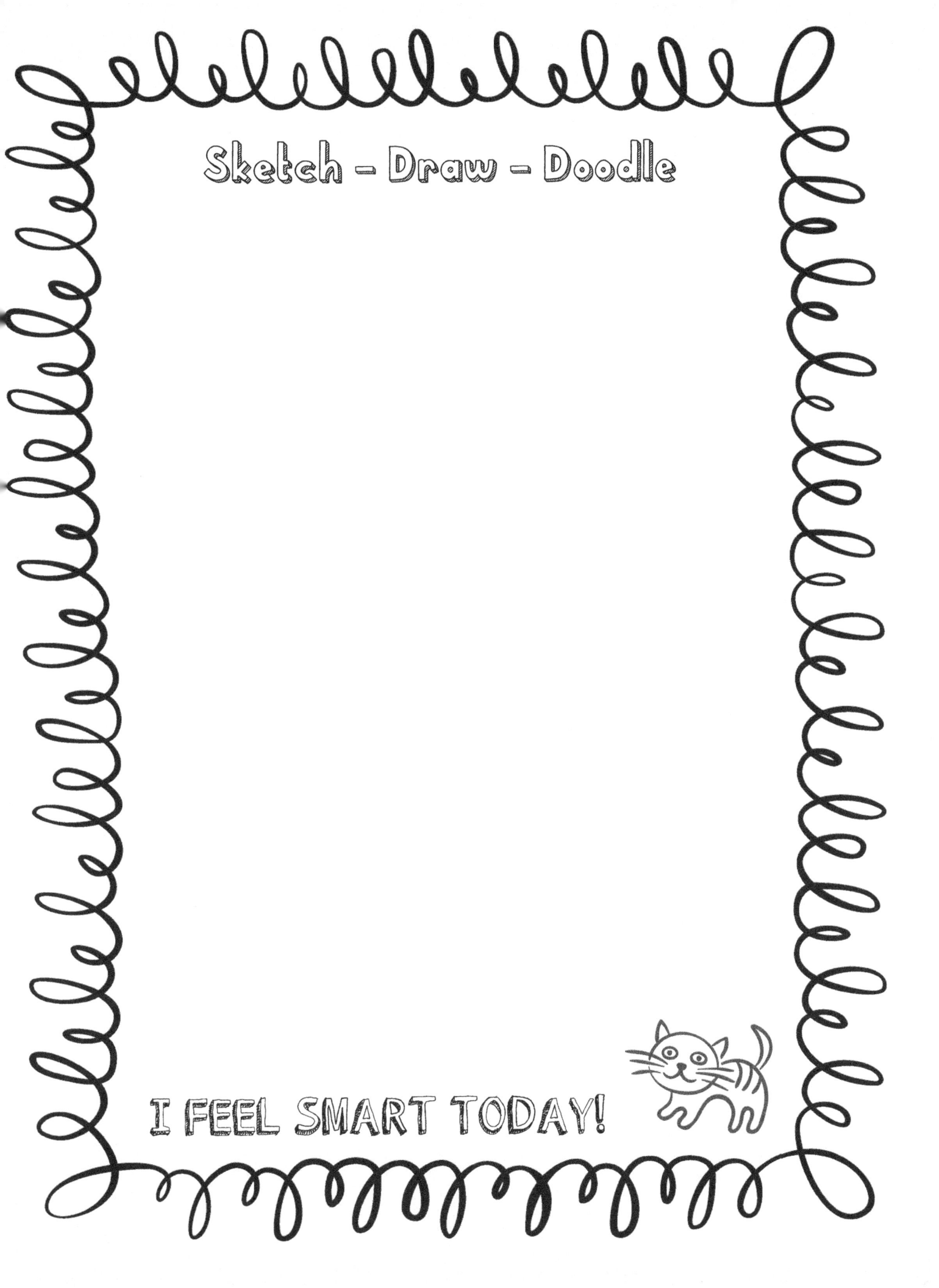

Sketch - Draw - Doodle

I FEEL SMART TODAY!

Sketch - Draw - Doodle

I FEEL GRATEFUL TODAY!

Sketch - Draw - Doodle

I FEEL AMAZING TODAY!

Sketch - Draw - Doodle

I FEEL HAPPY TODAY!

Sketch - Draw - Doodle

I FEEL COOL TODAY!

Sketch – Draw – Doodle

I FEEL GOOD TODAY!

Sketch - Draw - Doodle

I FEEL CREATIVE TODAY!

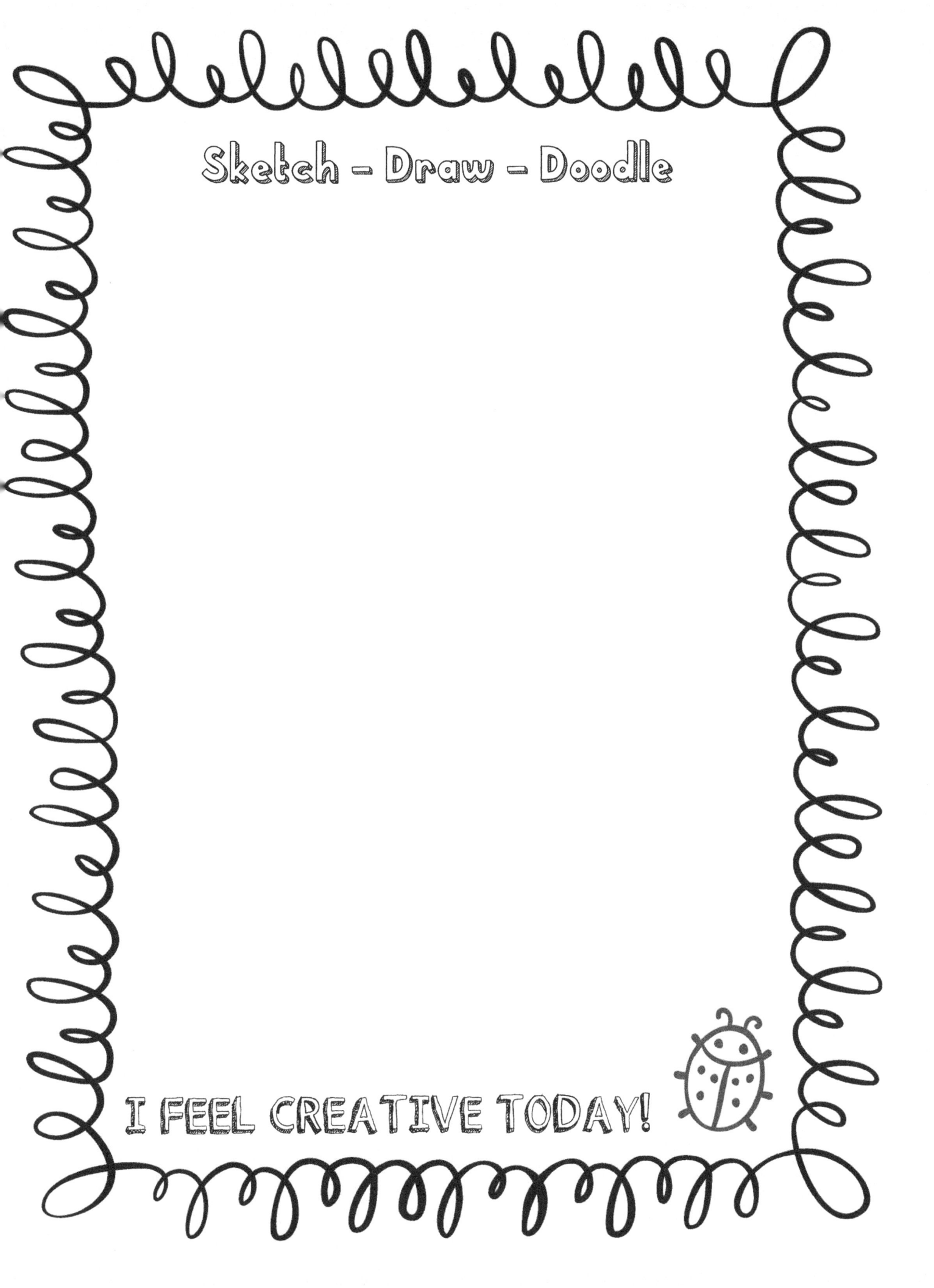

Sketch – Draw – Doodle

I FEEL PLAYFUL TODAY!

Sketch - Draw - Doodle

I FEEL STRONG TODAY!

Sketch - Draw - Doodle

I FEEL AMAZING TODAY!

Sketch - Draw - Doodle

I FEEL COOL TODAY!

Sketch – Draw – Doodle

I FEEL GREAT TODAY!

Sketch - Draw - Doodle

I FEEL GOOD TODAY!

Sketch – Draw – Doodle

I FEEL AWESOME TODAY!

Sketch - Draw - Doodle

I FEEL SMART TODAY!

Sketch - Draw - Doodle

I FEEL CREATIVE TODAY!

Sketch - Draw - Doodle

I FEEL GOOD TODAY!

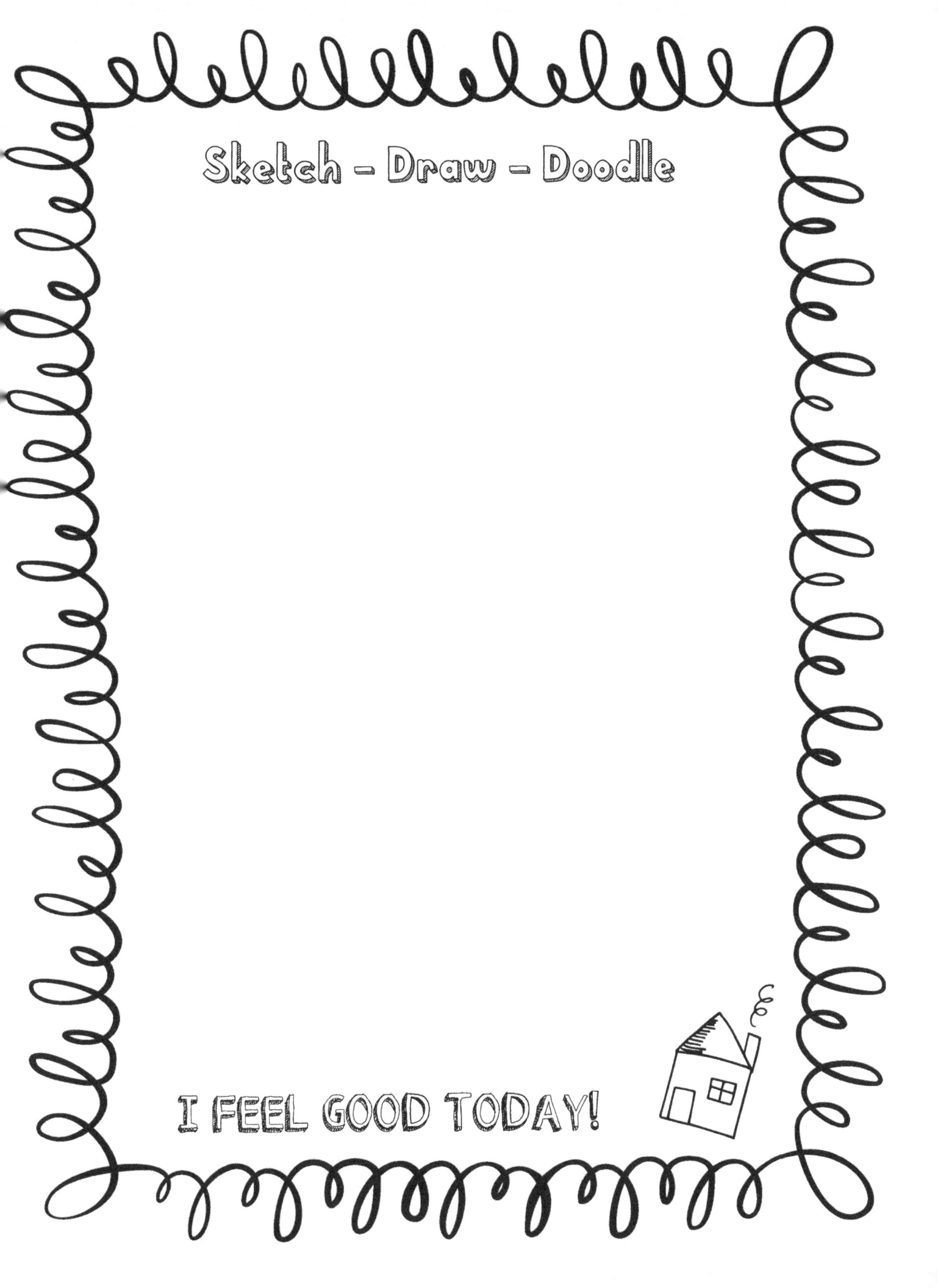

Sketch – Draw – Doodle

I FEEL HAPPY TODAY!

Sketch - Draw - Doodle

I FEEL CREATIVE TODAY!

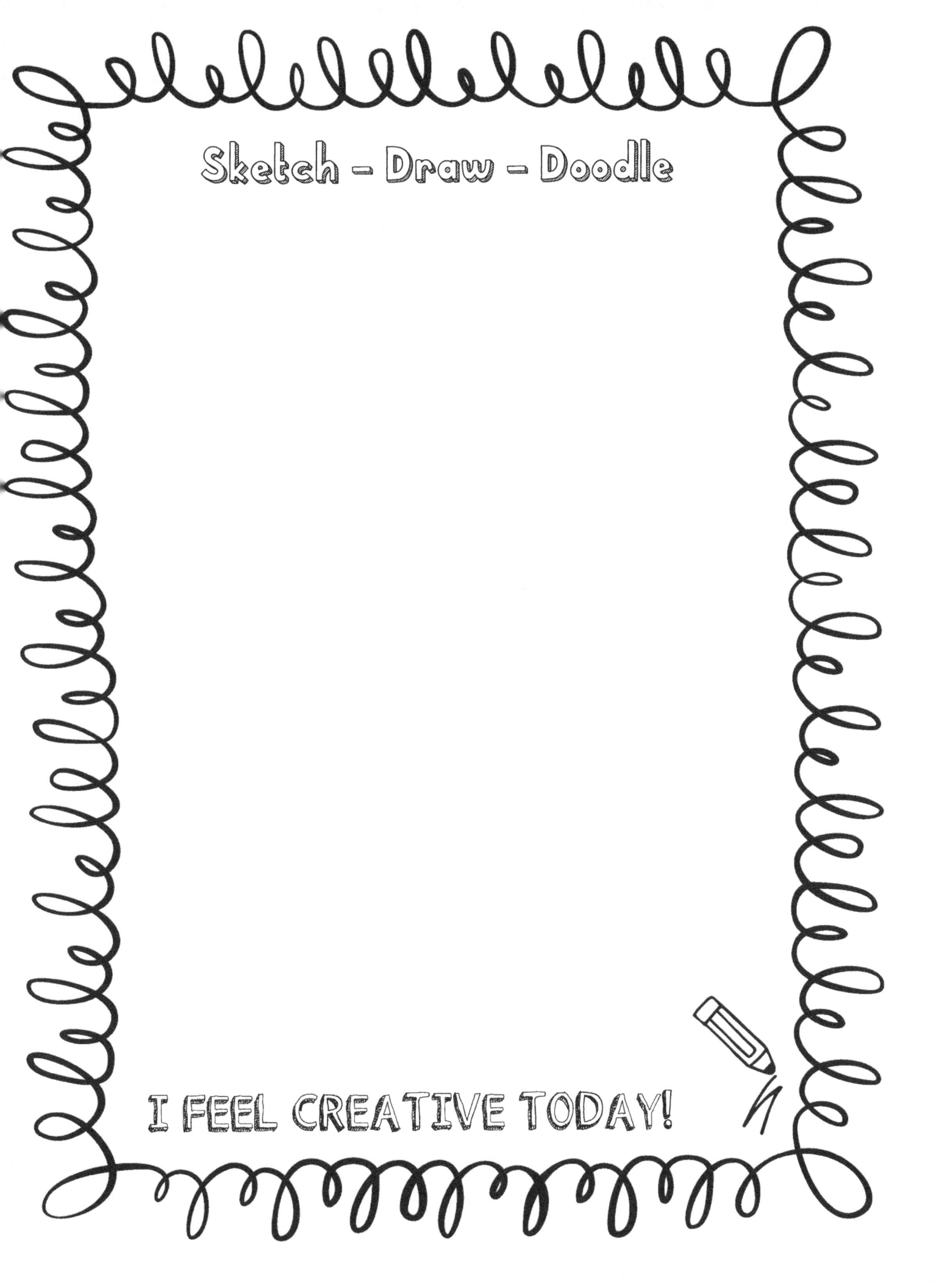

Sketch – Draw – Doodle

I FEEL AWESOME TODAY!

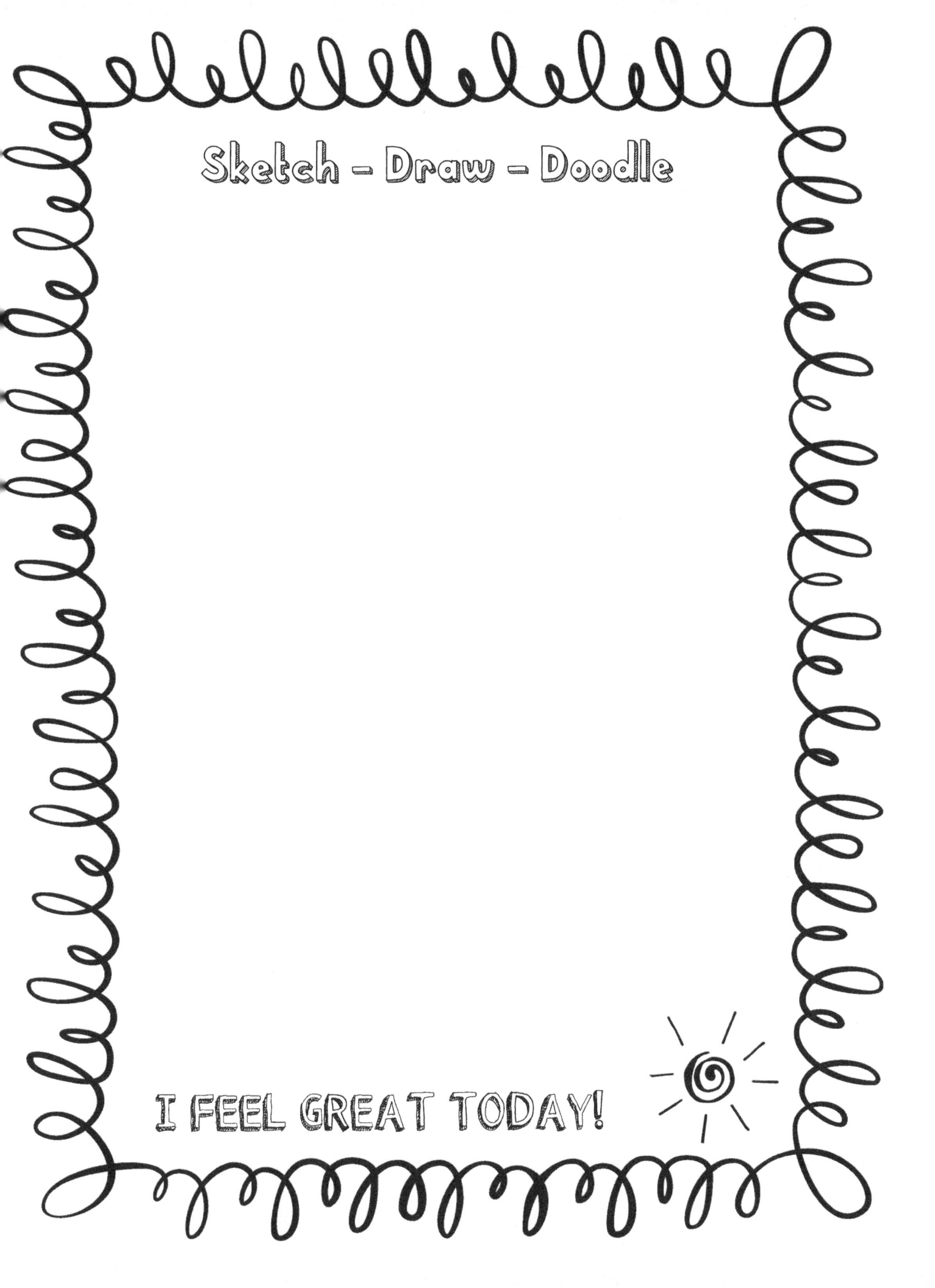

Sketch - Draw - Doodle

I FEEL GREAT TODAY!

Sketch – Draw – Doodle

I FEEL HAPPY TODAY!

Sketch - Draw - Doodle

I FEEL GREAT TODAY!

Sketch – Draw – Doodle

I FEEL STRONG TODAY!

Sketch - Draw - Doodle

I FEEL COOL TODAY!

Sketch – Draw – Doodle

I FEEL STRONG TODAY!

Sketch - Draw - Doodle

I FEEL GREAT TODAY!

Sketch – Draw – Doodle

I FEEL HAPPY TODAY!

Sketch - Draw - Doodle

I FEEL GOOD TODAY!

Sketch - Draw - Doodle

I FEEL AWESOME TODAY!

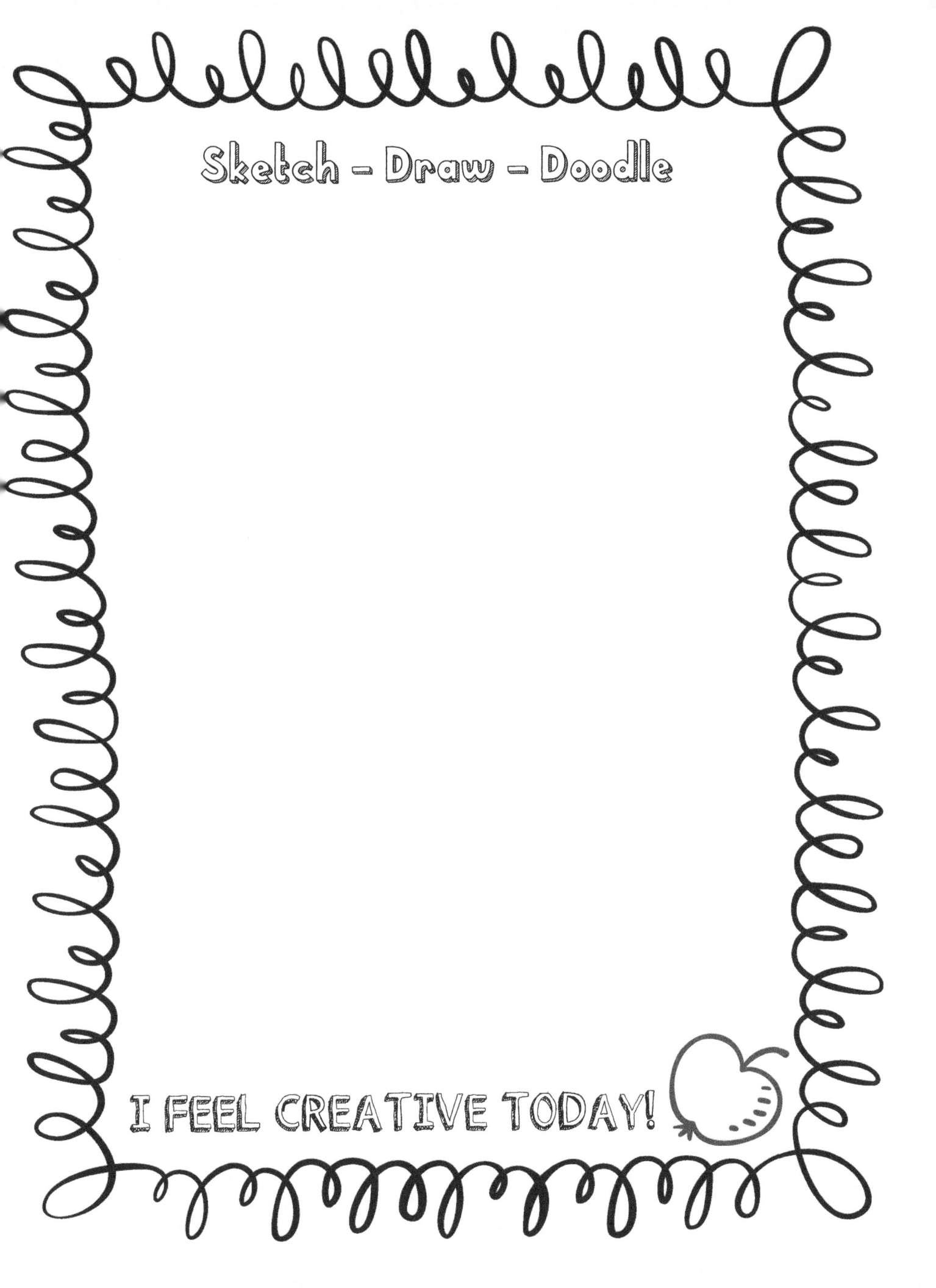

Sketch - Draw - Doodle

I FEEL CREATIVE TODAY!

Sketch – Draw – Doodle

I FEEL HAPPY TODAY!

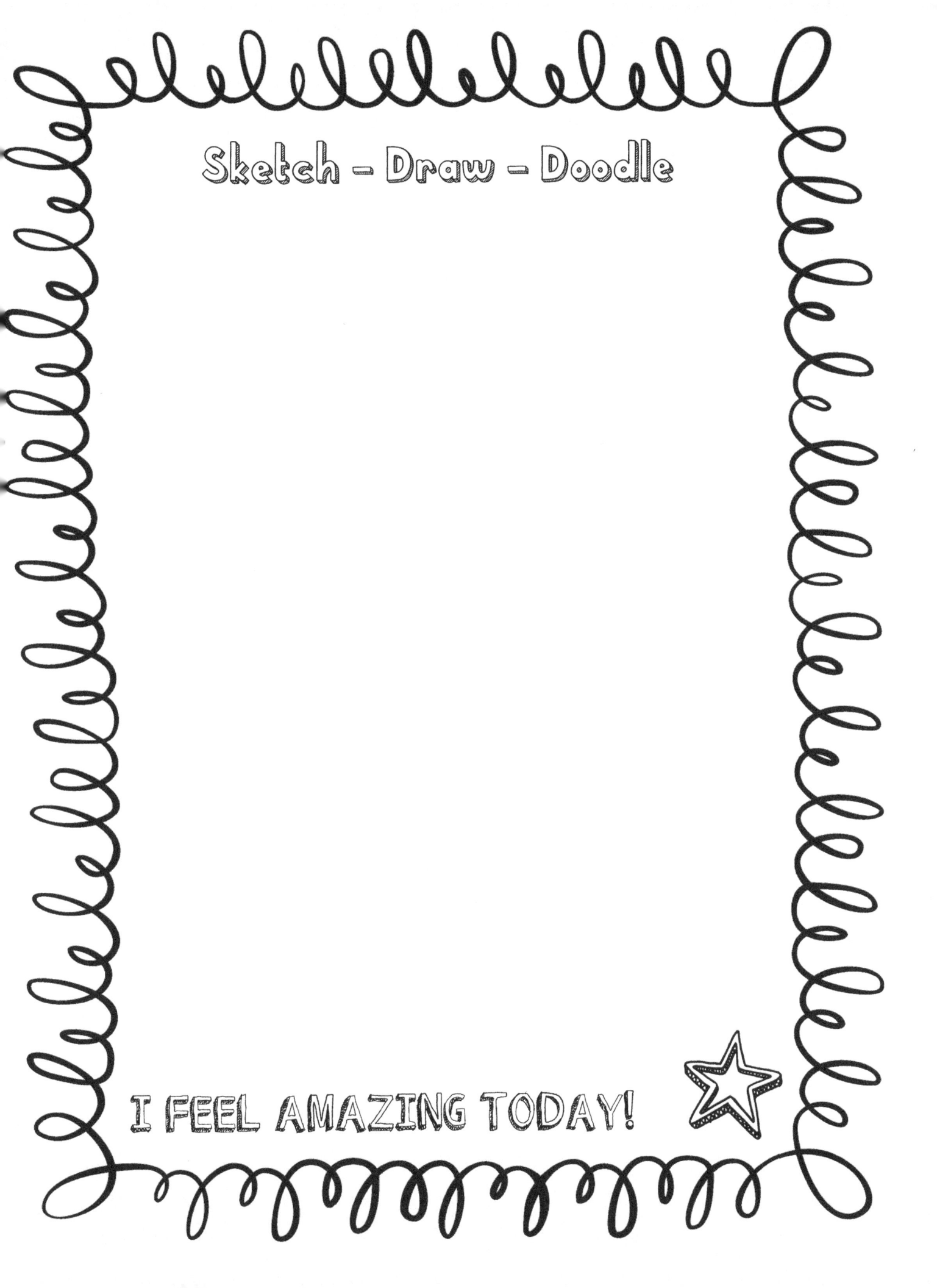

Sketch – Draw – Doodle

I FEEL AMAZING TODAY!

Sketch – Draw – Doodle

I FEEL SMART TODAY!

CREATIVE JOURNALS FACTORY

DESIGNED BY CREATIVE SKETCHBOOKS STUDIO
FOR **CREATIVE JOURNALS FACTORY.**

THANK YOU WE HOPE YOU LIKED YOUR SKETCHBOOK
PLEASE WRITE YOUR REVIEW, IT MEANS A LOT TO US!
Thank you!

FIND OTHER BEAUTIFUL JOURNALS, DIARIES AND NOTEBOOKS AT:

www.CreativeJournalsFactory.com

JOURNALS - DIARIES - NOTEBOOKS - COLORING BOOKS

Made in the USA
Monee, IL
28 January 2021